Animal Epitaphs

J. Patrick Lewis and Jane Yolen
Illustrated by Jeffrey Stewart Timmins

ini Charlesbridge

Contents

Last Laughs 5

Good-bye to a Rowdy Rooster 6

Chicken Crosses Over 6

Hen's Last Cluck 7

Tough Turkey 7

No Longer Horsing Around 8

Ciao, Cow 9

Final Pound for a Hound 10

Grabby Tabby 11

Katydidn't 12

Firefly's Final Flight 13

Flickering Moth 13

The Last of a Staggering Stag 14

For a Bear, Barely There 15

Woodpecker's Last Hole 16

Mourning a Dove 17

Owl Be Seeing You 17

Cooked Goose 18

Swan Song 19

For a Frog: Not a Hoppy Ending 20

Double-crossed Newt 21

Blue Whale Blues 22

A Narwhal, Foiled Again 23

Not Gone on Porpoise 23

A Swordfish's Pointed End 24

Barracuda's Bite-size Demise 25

R.I.P. (Really Inattentive Piranha) 26

Eel Seals the Final Deal 27

End of a Rattling Battler 28

Hasta Mañana, Iguana 29

An Infirm Worm 30

4

Last Laughs

Here at Amen
Creature Corners,
beasties weep
like misty mourners,
but when they read
an epitaph,
it always brings them
one last laugh.
Forget the hankies.
Read the words
of bugs and fishes,
beasts and birds.
They know it's not
all gloom and doom
that's written
once upon a tomb.

Good—bye to a Rowdy Rooster

Too cocky by far,
he head-butted a car.

Chicken Crosses Over

She never found the answer
to the age-old question,
Why did the chicken cross the ro—?

6

Hen's Last Cluck

The end of her day
was in fowl play.

Tough Turkey

Sorry, no leftovers.

No Longer Horsing Around

First he was just
a little hoarse,
then the fever
took its course.

Ciao, Cow

This grave is peaceful,
the tombstone shaded,
but I'm not here—
I've been cream-ated.

9

Final Pound for a Hound

Once he dug holes in the lawn;
now he's there himself,
dog-gone.

Grabby Tabby

She always loved
a good yarn.

11

Katydidn't

The car wouldn't stop;
the car wouldn't yield.
The bug couldn't hop
the front windshield.

12

Firefly's Final Flight

Lights out.

Flickering Moth

Here lies a moth
without a name,
who lived by the fire
and died by the flame.

The Last of a Staggering Stag

Win some.

Lose some.

Venison.

For a Bear, Barely There

He crawled inside
to hibernate
and reach his goal
of losing weight.
He missed the spring,
the summer, fall . . .
having eaten
not at all.
Another winter
swirled outside,
so he—
with overbearing pride—
lay right back down
and barely sighed.
At least,
he thought
before he died,
I tried.

15

Woodpecker's Last Hole

One peck too many
severed a limb,
and that was the end
of impeccable him.

Mourning a Dove

Go, wing,
go, wing . . .
gone.

Owl Be Seeing You

Hit by a pellet
some other owl cast,
he asked, "Who?" quietly
as he passed.

Cooked Goose

He was Canada born
and Canada bred,
and here he lies—
Canada dead.

18

Swan Song

A simple song.
It wasn't long.

For a Frog: Not a Hoppy Ending

In his pond,
he peacefully soaked,
then, ever so quietly
croaked.

Double-crossed Newt

Little newt,
so small,
so fine,
so squashed
beneath
the crossing
sign.

caution
newts

21

Blue Whale Blues

She sang a melody,
two continents apart,
so long and sad, the echo
broke her heart.

A Narwhal, Foiled Again

His end was hard,
when not *en garde*.

Not Gone on Porpoise

She wasn't sure which—
butterfly, breast, or back—
but she had a stroke.

A Swordfish's Pointed End

I fought a shark,
up to a point.
Shark left his mark—
nose out of joint.

24

Barracuda's Bite-size Demise

My teeth were vicious;
my bite was hateful.
A great white met me—
the date was fateful.
The shark was hungry,
and I was baitful.

R.I.P. (Really Inattentive Piranha)

The second-sharpest
teeth in the river.

26

Eel Seals the Final Deal

You really know
how bad you feel
when you become
extremely eel.
There was a time
when I swam by you
that I could still
electrify you.

End of a Rattling Battler

Shake,
death rattle,
and roll
over.

8

Hasta Mañana, Iguana

I wrestled tumbleweed,
just for practice,
then I got pinned by
a saguaro cactus!

29

An Infirm Worm

To all the worms who've fed and fed
upon remains, you'll soon be dead.
Those who have the final laugh
will read these words on your behalf.
Here inside your earthbound tomb,
you'll find you've no more wiggle room.

For Tim and Mary, still kicking—J. P. L.

For Alison and David, who love to laugh—J. Y.

For Muggins and Simon: wherever you are,
I hope there are squirrels—J. S. T.

Published by Charlesbridge
85 Main Street
Watertown, MA 02472
(617) 926-0329
www.charlesbridge.com

Library of Congress Cataloging-in-Publication Data
Lewis, J. Patrick.
    Last laughs : animal epitaphs / J. Patrick Lewis and Jane Yolen ;
illustrated by Jeffrey Stewart Timmins.
       p. cm.
    ISBN 978-1-58089-260-5 (reinforced for library use)
    ISBN 978-1-60734-453-7 (ebook)
1. Animals—Juvenile humor. 2. Animals—Juvenile poetry. I. Yolen, Jane. II. Timmins,
Jeffrey Stewart. III. Title.
PN6231.A5L49 2011
818'.602—dc23   2011025702

Printed in Singapore
(hc) 10 9 8 7 6 5 4 3 2

Illustrations made using Adobe Photoshop, ink, and gouache on cold-pressed paper
Display type and text type set in Tuzonie and Dante MT
Color separations by KHL Chroma Graphics, Singapore
Printed October 2012 by Imago in Singapore
Production supervision by Brian G. Walker
Designed by Martha MacLeod Sikkema